Changes All Around Us

Monica Halpern

Contents

What Is Change?

Everything around you changes in some way. Some changes happen quickly. Have you ever seen a warm, sunny day change suddenly into a cold, rainy day? Changes that happen quickly, like changes in weather, are changes you can see happening.

Some changes happen slowly. Mountains, for example, are slowly worn down by wind and rain. You can't see high mountains changing as you look at them, but they are changing slowly. Over time, they won't be as tall.

Both fast and slow changes are happening in this picture. What changes can you find?

Some changes happen over and over again. These type of changes are called cycles. Seasons change in cycles. The seasons also bring changes to life on Earth. Do you wear heavy clothes in winter and light clothes in summer? You are changing how you dress as the seasons change.

Animals and people go through cycles, too. These cycles are called life cycles. A life cycle means an animal is born, grows up, and then dies. All animals and people go through changes during their life cycles.

This young fox will go through many changes as it grows into a full-grown fox like its mother.

Changes Over Time

Let's take a hike through the mountains. On the hike, you'll see things that have changed quickly and things that have changed slowly over time. Put on your hiking boots and let's get going!

From Rocks to Flowers

You're hiking through the mountains on a warm spring day. You notice beautiful flowers growing on the hillside. Have flowers and green grass always grown here? No! Long ago, this lush, green hillside was mostly rocks. How did this change occur?

Long ago, rain fell on the hillside. Winds wore down the rocks. Little by little, wind and rain broke up the rocks.

Weather wears down the rocks.

Eventually, small plants started to grow on top of the cracked, worn rock. The plants and bits of rock formed soil. In time, the soil got thicker.

Next, earthworms and other small animals moved in. These animals squirmed around in the dirt, making it a good place for plants to grow. That's how that rocky hillside became covered with flowers.

Over time, soil forms.

Then, flowers grow in the soil.

A River Makes Changes

You are now at the bottom of a deep, narrow valley with steep sides. It's called a canyon. A wide river flows through it.

Look up at the steep rocky sides of the canyon. Long ago, this canyon was not here. It was all solid rock. How was this canyon formed?

The river started carving out this canyon five million years ago! At first, the river flowed along the surface of the land. It flowed over the same area for a long period of time. As it flowed, it wore down the rock along its banks. It formed a channel, a kind of path through the rock.

As time passed, the channel became deeper and deeper. Eventually, the rock formed steep cliffs along its sides. It took a very long time for the river to change the rock. You couldn't see it happen. Even today, the river at the bottom of the canyon is changing the canyon. But the changes are slow and hard to see.

Over time, the river wore down
the rocks and made this canyon.

Quick Changes

Now you are hiking in a wooded area. Parts of it look gray and lifeless. Nothing seems to be moving. Here and there, you can see black, dead trees. Was it always like this?

Forest Fire!

About a year ago, this forest was green. It was filled with tall trees and thick bushy plants. Lots of animals lived here, too. Then, one hot, summer day, a storm moved in. Lightning struck a tree and some bushes, setting them on fire. Soon the forest was in flames.

Firefighters worked to stop the fire, but the fire burned for days. Eventually, the fire burned out. But now, the forest looks dead. In just a few days, the lush, green forest was changed into this gray land. Will it ever change back?

Yes, a forest will grow here again. But it will take 50 to 100 years for it to grow back completely!

The forest looked like this ten years after the fire.

Weather Changes

Your boots kick up dust as you hike along the dry path. It's warm and sunny out here. But you notice a cool breeze and see clouds moving in.

Now you hear a low rumble. What is it? It's thunder! Rain pours down from the sky, soaking everything, including you! You put on your raincoat as quickly as you can, but you're already very wet. You weren't ready for this fast change in weather!

Weather can change from day to day, and even from hour to hour. Less than an hour ago, it was a warm, sunny day. But now the sky is dark. The air has cooled and the rain pours down as if it will never stop!

Clouds slowly move in on a sunny day.

After a while, the rain slows down and then stops. Water drips from the trees. The path is now a small, muddy river as the water drains off into the soaking grass. The sun is peeking through the clouds. Soon, it will be warm again, and the land will become dry.

After a heavy rain, the sky begins to clear.

Cycles

The sun is setting. Soon it will be dark. It's time to set up camp for the night. As night falls, you see the forest in a new way. The cycle of day changing to night brings changes to the forest.

Day Changes To Night

Early this morning, as the sun rose, you may have noticed the ground was wet with morning dew. The air was cool. Birds were just waking, chirping to each other. Insects called out, too. Some animals were beginning their day, just like you were.

Sunrise

By noon, the day was warm. The sun was high in the sky. Insects flew around as you hiked along the path. Birds flew and called to each other. Animals moved quickly from place to place in search of food.

Now, it is night. The sky is dark and filled with stars. The sun has set and the moon is bright. Some animals are preparing for sleep, but others are just waking. They will now begin their hunt for food. Soon, it will be morning again. It's time to sleep.

Sunset

The Seasons Change

Every year, the four seasons arrive in the same order—spring, summer, fall, and winter. The seasons form a cycle.

Changing seasons have a major effect on living things. In the spring and summer, days are long and the weather is mild. Plants grow lush and green, and animals spend time eating and reproducing.

Summer

Fall

In the fall, the days become cooler and shorter. Plants begin shedding their leaves. Some animals begin storing food and preparing shelters for winter. Other animals, like birds, move to warmer places until spring returns.

In the winter, the days are short and cold. Some animals hibernate. During hibernation, an animal spends most of its time resting in a cozy shelter. Plants seem to shrivel up and die during winter months. But they are resting. In spring, the plants grow buds and become green again.

Winter

Spring

Life Cycles

We've been hiking for some time now. Let's stop for a while by the pond. Look at those tiny frogs in the water. And big frogs, too! Frogs, like all living things, go through changes as they grow. These changes are called a life cycle. A life cycle means an animal is born, grows up, and eventually dies.

From Tadpole to Frog

Many frogs begin their lives as tiny, black eggs floating in water. After a while, tadpoles hatch from the eggs.

Tadpoles live underwater. They have tails and large bodies. Over time, the tadpoles change. They grow front and back legs. Their tails get shorter. Soon, their tails will disappear.

The adult frog spends lots of time out of the pond. In winter, the frog will hibernate. In spring, it will find food and a mate. Then, the female frog will lay eggs in the pond. And more tadpoles will hatch.

An adult frog can live in the water and on the land. It must come out of the water to breathe.

A tadpole lives in the water. It has a tail and swims in the water.

As it grows, a tadpole changes. It grows legs. It also develops lungs that allow it to breathe out of the water.

From Baby to Adult

It's time to hike back towards the picnic area. You see a group of friends and their families enjoying a picnic. You smile at a baby toddling towards his grandmother.

Then, you realize that people go through life cycles, too, just like frogs and all other living things. People change as they grow older.

Think of how much you've changed since you were a baby. You are still changing and growing. In a few years, you will be taller. Your skills will change.

When you are an adult, you will be fully grown. You will be able to take care of yourself. You may want to start a family of your own. Maybe one day, you will smile as your grandchild toddles towards you.

Changes All Around You

What a great hiking trip! You've seen changes all around you—slow changes in mountains and canyons, and fast changes from forest fires and weather. You've seen changes happen in the cycles of days and seasons, and in the life cycles of frogs and people.

All of these changes are called natural changes because they happen without the help of people. But people can cause changes, too. These are called human-made changes.

Natural changes and human-made changes happen everywhere, not just in the forest and mountains. Look around you and you will notice changes in your own community. Which changes are natural and which are human-made? Which changes happened slowly and which happened quickly?

What human-made and natural changes can you see in the picture?

Index